The Writings of Julius Africanus

The Writings of Julius Africanus

Julius Africanus

The Writings of Julius Africanus

© Lighthouse Publishing 2023

Written by: Julius Africanus (AD 200 - 245)
Translated by: Rev. Ernest Wallis, Ph.D.(1820 – 1910)
Updated into Modern U.S English: A.M. Overett (b.1960)

All rights reserved. Without limiting the rights under copyright reserved above, no part of this publication may be reproduced, stored in a retrieval system, or transmitted, in any form or by any means (electronic, mechanical, photocopying, recording or otherwise), without the prior written permission of the copyright owner of this book.

Published by
Lighthouse Publishing
SAN 257-4330
228 Freedom Parkway
Hoschton, GA 30548
United States of America

www.lighthousechristianpublishing.com

Introductory Notice
to
Julius Africanus.

[a.d. 200–232–245.] In a former volume, strengthened by a word from Archbishop Usher, I have not hesitated to claim for Theophilus of Antioch a primary place among Christian chronologists. It is no detraction from the fame of our author to admit this, and truth requires it. But the great Alexandrian school must again come into view when we speak of any considerable achievements, among early Christian writers, in this important element of all biblical, in fact, all historical, science. Africanus was a pupil of Heraclas, and we must therefore date his pupilage in Alexandria before a.d. 232, when Dionysius succeeded Heraclas in the presidency of that school. It appears that in a.d. 226 he was performing some duty on behalf of Emmaus (Nicopolis) in Palestine; but Heraclas, who had acted subordinately as Origen's assistant as early as a.d. 218, could not have become the head of the school, even provisionally, till after Origen's unhappy ordination. Let us assume the period of our author's attending the school under Heraclas to be between a.d. 228 and a.d. 232, however. We may then venture to reckon his birth as *circa* a.d. 200. And, if he became "bishop of Emmaus," it could hardly have been before the year 240, when he was of ripe age and experience. He adds additional luster to the age of Gregory Thaumaturgus and Dionysius, as well as to that of their common mother in letters and theology, the already ancient academy of Pantænus and of Clement. His reviving credit in modern times has been largely due to the learned criticism of Dr. Routh, to whose edition of these Fragments the student must necessarily apply. Their chief interest arises from the important specimen which treats of the difficult question of the genealogies of our Lord contained in the evangelists. For a succinct statement of the points involved, and for a candid concession that they were not preserved to meet what modern curiosity would prefer to see established, I know of nothing more satisfactory than the commentary of Wordsworth, from which I have borrowed almost wholly one of my elucidations.

The reader will remember the specimen of our author's critical judgment which is given with the works of Origen. He differed with that great author, and the Church Catholic has sustained his judgment as just. I regret that the Edinburgh editors thought it necessary to make the *Letter to Origen concerning the Apocryphal Book of Susannah* a mere preface to Origen's answer. It might have been quoted there as a preface; but it is too important not to be included here, with the other fragments of his noble contributions to primitive Christian literature.

It does not clearly appear, from the Edinburgh edition, who the translator is; but here follows the

Translator's Introductory Notice.

The principal facts known to us in the life of Africanus are derived from himself and the *Chronicon* of Eusebius. He says of himself that he went to Alexandria on account of the fame of Heraclas. In the *Chronicon*, under the year 226, it is stated that "Nicopolis in Palestine, which formerly bore the name of Emmaus, was built, Africanus, the author of the *Chronology*, acting as ambassador on behalf of it, and having the charge of it." Dionysius Bar-Salibi speaks of Africanus as bishop of Emmaus.

Eusebius describes Africanus as being the author of a work called κεστοί. Suidas says that this book detailed various kinds of cures, consisting of charms and written forms, and such like. Some have supposed that such a work is not likely to have been written by a Christian writer: they appeal also to the fact that no notice is taken of the κεστοί by Jerome in his notice of Africanus, nor by Rufinus in his translation of Eusebius. They therefore deem the clause in Eusebius an interpolation, and they suppose that two bore the name of Africanus,—one the author of the κεστοί, the other the Christian writer. Suidas identifies them, says that he was surnamed Sextus, and that he was a Libyan philosopher.

The works ascribed to Africanus, beside the *Cesti*, are the following:—

1. *Five Books of Chronology*. Photius says of this work, that it was concise, but omitted nothing of importance. It began with the cosmogony of Moses, and went down to the advent of Christ. It summarized also the events from the time of Christ to the reign of the Emperor Macrinus.

2. A very famous letter to Aristides, in which he endeavored to reconcile the apparent discrepancies in the genealogies of Christ given by Matthew and Luke.

3. A letter to Origen, in which he endeavored to prove that the story of Susanna in Daniel was a forgery. A translation of this letter has been given with the *Works of Origen*.

The Acts of Symphorosa and her Seven Sons are attributed in the mss. to Africanus; but no ancient writer speaks of him as the author of this work.

The Extant Writings of Julius Africanus.

I.—The Epistle to Aristides.

I.

[Africanus on the Genealogy in the Holy Gospels.—Some indeed incorrectly allege that this discrepant enumeration and mixing of the names both of priestly men, as they think, and royal, was made properly, in order that Christ might be shown rightfully to be both Priest and King; as if any one disbelieved this, or had any other hope than this, that Christ is the High Priest of His Father, who presents our prayers to Him, and a supramundane King, who rules by the Spirit those whom He has delivered, a cooperator in the government of all things. And this is announced to us not by the catalogue of the tribes, nor by the mixing of the registered generations, but by the patriarchs and prophets. Let us not therefore descend to such religious trifling as to establish the kingship and priesthood of Christ by the interchanges of the names. For the priestly tribe of Levi, too, was allied with the kingly tribe of Juda, through the circumstance that Aaron married Elizabeth the sister of Naasson, and that Eleazar again married the daughter of Phatiel, and begat children. The evangelists, therefore, would thus have spoken falsely, affirming what was not truth, but a fictitious commendation. And for this reason the one traced the pedigree of Jacob the father of Joseph from David through Solomon; the other traced that of Heli also, though in a different way, the father of Joseph, from Nathan the son of David. And they ought not indeed to have been ignorant that both orders of the ancestors enumerated are the generation of David, the royal tribe of

Juda. For if Nathan was a prophet, so also was Solomon, and so too the father of both of them; and there were prophets belonging to many of the tribes, but priests belonging to none of the tribes, save the Levites only. To no purpose, then, is this fabrication of theirs. Nor shall an assertion of this kind prevail in the Church of Christ against the exact truth, so as that a lie should be contrived for the praise and glory of Christ. For who does not know that most holy word of the apostle also, who, when he was preaching and proclaiming the resurrection of our Savior, and confidently affirming the truth, said with great fear, "If any say that Christ is not risen, and we assert and have believed this, and both hope for and preach that very thing, we are false witnesses of God, in alleging that He raised up Christ, whom He raised not up?" And if he who glorifies God the Father is thus afraid lest he should seem a false witness in narrating a marvelous fact, how should not he be justly afraid, who tries to establish the truth by a false statement, preparing an untrue opinion? For if the generations are different, and trace down no genuine seed to Joseph, and if all has been stated only with the view of establishing the position of Him who was to be born—to confirm the truth, namely, that He who was to be would be king and priest, there being at the same time no proof given, but the dignity of the words being brought down to a feeble hymn,—it is evident that no praise accrues to God from that, since it is a falsehood, but rather judgment returns on him who asserts it, because he vaunts an unreality as though it were reality. Therefore, that we may expose the ignorance also of him who speaks thus, and prevent anyone from stumbling at this folly, I shall set forth the true history of these matters.]

II.

For whereas in Israel the names of their generations were enumerated either according to nature or according to law,—according to nature, indeed, by the succession of legitimate offspring, and according to law whenever another raised up children to the name of a brother dying childless; for because no clear hope of resurrection was yet given them, they had a representation of the future promise in a kind of mortal resurrection, with the view of perpetuating the name of one deceased;—whereas, then, of those entered in this genealogy, some succeeded by legitimate descent as son to father, while others begotten in one family were introduced to another in name, mention is therefore made of both—of those who were progenitors in fact, and of those who were so only in name. Thus neither of the evangelists is in error, as the one reckons by nature and the other by law. For the several generations, viz., those descending from Solomon and those from Nathan, were so intermingled by the raising up of children to the childless, and by second marriages, and the raising up of seed, that the same persons are quite justly reckoned to belong at one time to the one, and at another to the other, i.e., to their reputed or to their actual fathers. And hence it is that both these accounts are true, and come down to Joseph, with considerable intricacy indeed, but yet quite accurately.

III.

But in order that what I have said may be made evident, I shall explain the inter- change of the generations. If we reckon the generations from David through Solomon, Matthan is found to be the third from the end, who begat Jacob the father of Joseph. But if, with

Luke, we reckon them from Nathan the son of David, in like manner the third from the end is Melchi, whose son was Heli the father of Joseph. For Joseph was the son of Heli, the son of Melchi. As Joseph, therefore, is the object proposed to us, we have to show how it is that each is represented as his father, both Jacob as descending from Solomon, and Heli as descending from Nathan: first, how these two, Jacob and Heli, were brothers; and then also how the fathers of these, Matthan and Melchi, being of different families, are shown to be the grandfathers of Joseph. Well, then, Matthan and Melchi, having taken the same woman to wife in succession, begat children who were uterine brothers, as the law did not prevent a widow, whether such by divorce or by the death of her husband, from marrying another. By Estha, then—for such is her name according to tradition—Matthan first, the descendant of Solomon, begets Jacob; and on Matthan's death, Melchi, who traces his descent back to Nathan, being of the same tribe but of another family, having married her, as has been already said, had a son Heli. Thus, then, we shall find Jacob and Heli uterine brothers, though of different families. And of these, the one Jacob having taken the wife of his brother Heli, who died childless, begat by her the third, Joseph—his son by nature and by account. Whence also it is written, "And Jacob begat Joseph." But according to law he was the son of Heli, for Jacob his brother raised up seed to him. Wherefore also the genealogy deduced through him will not be made void, which the Evangelist Matthew in his enumeration gives thus: "And Jacob begat Joseph." But Luke, on the other hand, says, "Who was the son, as was supposed (for this, too, he adds), of Joseph, the son of Heli, the son of Melchi." For it was not possible more distinctly to state the generation according to law; and thus in this mode of generation he has entirely omitted the word "begat" to the very end, carrying back the genealogy by way of conclusion to Adam and to God.

V.

Nor indeed is this incapable of proof, neither is it a rash conjecture. For the kinsmen of the Savior after the flesh, whether to magnify their own origin or simply to state the fact, but at all events speaking truth, have also handed down the following account: Some Idumean robbers attacking Ascalon, a city of Palestine, besides other spoils which they took from a temple of Apollo, which was built near the walls, carried off captive one Antipater, son of a certain Herod, a servant of the temple. And as the priest was not able to pay the ransom for his son, Antipater was brought up in the customs of the Idumeans, and afterwards enjoyed the friendship of Hyrcanus, the high priest of Judea. And being sent on an embassy to Pompey on behalf of Hyrcanus, and having restored to him the kingdom which was being wasted by Aristobulus his brother, he was so fortunate as to obtain the title of procurator of Palestine. And when Antipater was treacherously slain through envy of his great good fortune, his son Herod succeeded him, who was afterwards appointed king of Judea under Antony and Augustus by a decree of the senate. His sons were Herod and the other tetrarchs. These accounts are given also in the histories of the Greeks.

V.

But as up to that time the genealogies of the Hebrews had been registered in the public archives, and those, too, which were traced back to the proselytes—as, for example, to Achior the Ammanite, and Ruth the Moabitess, and those who left Egypt along with the Israelites, and intermarried with them—Herod, knowing that the lineage of the Israelites contributed nothing to him, and goaded by the consciousness of his ignoble birth, burned the registers of their families. This he did, thinking that he would appear to be of noble birth, if no one else could trace back his descent by the public register to the patriarchs or proselytes, and to that mixed race called *georæ*. A few, however, of the studious, having private records of their own, either by remembering the names or by getting at them in some other way from the archives, pride themselves in preserving the memory of their noble descent; and among these happen to be those already mentioned, called *desposyni*, on account of their connection with the family of the Savior. And these coming from Nazara and Cochaba, Judean villages, to other parts of the country, set forth the above-named genealogy as accurately as possible from the Book of Days. Whether then, the case stand thus or not, no one could discover a more obvious explanation, according to my own opinion and that of any sound judge. And let this suffice us for the matter, although it is not supported by testimony, because we have nothing more satisfactory or true to allege upon it. The Gospel, however, in any case states the truth.

VI.

Matthan, descended from Solomon, begat Jacob. Matthan dying, Melchi, descended from Nathan, begat Heli by the same wife. Therefore Heli and Jacob are uterine brothers. Heli dying childless, Jacob raised up seed to him and begat Joseph, his own son by nature, but the son of Heli by law. Thus Joseph was the son of both.

II.—Narrative of Events Happening in Persia on the Birth of Christ.

The best introduction to this production will be the following preface, as given in Migne:—Many men of learning thus far have been of opinion that the narrative by Africanus of events happening in Persia on Christ's birth, is a fragment of that famous work which Sextus Julius Africanus, a Christian author of the third century after Christ, composed on the history of the world in the chronological order of events up to the reign of Macrinus, and presented in five books to Alexander, son of Mammæa, with the view of obtaining the restoration of his native town Emmaus. With the same expectation which I see incited Lambecius and his compendiator Nesselius, I, too, set myself with the greatest eagerness to go over the codices of our Electoral Library....But, as the common proverb goes, I found coals instead of treasure. This narrative, so far from its being to be ascribed to a writer well reputed by the common voice of antiquity, does not contain anything worthy of the genius of the chronographer Africanus. Wherefore, since by the unanimous testimony of the ancients he was a man of consummate learning and sharpest judgment, while the author of the *Cesti*, which also puts forward the name of Africanus, has been long marked by critics with the character either of anile credulity, or of a marvelous propensity to superstitious fancies, I can readily fall in with the opinion of those who think that he is a different person from the chronographer, and would ascribe this wretched production also to him. But, dear reader, on perusing these pages, if your indignation is not stirred against the man's rashness, you will at least join with me in laughing at his prodigious follies, and will learn, at the same time, that the testimonies of men most distinguished for learning are not to be rated so highly as to supersede personal examination when opportunity permits.

Events in Persia: On the Incarnation of Our Lord and God and Savior Jesus Christ.

Christ first of all became known from Persia. For nothing escapes the learned jurists of that country, who investigate all things with the utmost care. The facts, therefore, which are inscribed upon the golden plates, and laid up in the royal temples, I shall record; for it is from the temples there, and the priests connected with them, that the name of Christ has been heard of. Now there is a temple there to Juno, surpassing even the royal palace, which temple Cyrus, that prince instructed in all piety, built, and in which he dedicated in honor of the gods golden and silver statues, and adorned them with precious stones,—that I may not waste words in a profuse description of that ornamentation. Now about that time (as the records on the plates testify), the king having entered the temple, with the view of getting an interpretation of certain dreams, was addressed by the priest Prupupius thus: I congratulate thee, master: Juno has conceived. And the king, smiling, said to him, Has she who is dead conceived? And he said, Yes, she who was dead has come to life again, and begets life. And the king said, What is this? explain it to me. And he replied, In truth, master, the time for these things is at hand. For during the whole night the images, both of gods and goddesses, continued beating the ground, saying to each other, Come, let us congratulate Juno. And they say to me, Prophet, come forward; congratulate Juno, for she has been embraced. And I said, How can she be embraced who no longer exists? To which they reply, She has come to life again, and is no longer called Juno, but Urania. For the mighty Sol has embraced her. Then the goddesses say to the gods, making the matter plainer, *Pege* is she who is embraced; for did not Juno espouse an artificer? And the gods say, That she is rightly called *Pege*, we admit. Her name, moreover, is *Myria*; for she bears in her womb, as in the deep, a vessel of a myriad talents' burden. And as to this title Pege, let it be understood thus: This stream of water sends forth the perennial stream of spirit,—a stream containing but a single fish, taken with the hook of Divinity, and sustaining the whole world with its flesh as though it were in the sea. You have well said, She has an artificer [in espousal]; but by that espousal she does not bear an artificer on an equality with herself. For this artificer who is born, the son of the chief artificer, framed by his excellent skill the roof of the third heavens, and established by his word this lower world, with its threefold sphere of habitation.

Thus, then, the statues disputed with each other concerning Juno and Pege, and [at length] with one voice they said: When the day is finished, we all, gods and goddesses, shall know the matter clearly. Now, therefore, master, tarry for the rest of the day. For the matter shall certainly come to pass. For that which emerges is no common affair.

And when the king aboded there and watched the statues, the harpers of their own accord began to strike their harps, and the muses to sing; and whatsoever creatures were within, whether quadruped or fowl, in silver and gold, uttered their several voices. And as the king shuddered, and was filled with great fear, he was about to retire. For he could not endure the spontaneous tumult. The priest therefore said to him, Remain, O king, for the full revelation is at hand which the God of gods has chosen to declare to us.

And when these things were said, the roof was opened, and a bright star descended and stood above the pillar of Pege, and a voice was heard to this effect: Sovereign Pege, the mighty Son has sent me to make the announcement to you, and at the same time to do you service in parturition, designing blameless nuptials with you, O mother of the chief of all ranks of being, bride of the triune Deity. And the child begotten by extraordinary generation is called the *Beginning* and the *End*,—the beginning of salvation, and the end of perdition.

And when this word was spoken, all the statues fell upon their faces, that of Pege alone standing, on which also a royal diadem was found placed, having on its upper side a star set in a carbuncle and an emerald. And on its lower side the star rested.

And the king forthwith gave orders to bring in all the interpreters of prodigies, and the sages who were under his dominion. And when all the heralds sped with their proclamations, all these assembled in the temple. And when they saw the star above Pege, and the diadem with the star and the stone, and the statues lying on the floor, they said: O king, a root (off- spring) divine and princely has risen, bearing the image of the King of heaven and earth. For Pege-Myria is the daughter of the Bethlehemite Pege. And the diadem is the mark of a king, and the star is a celestial announcement of portents to fall on the earth. Out of Judah has arisen a kingdom which shall subvert all the memorials of the Jews. And the prostration of the gods upon the floor prefigured the end of their honor. For he who comes, being of more ancient dignity, shall displace all the recent. Now therefore, O king, send to Jerusalem. For you will find the Christ of the Omnipotent God borne in bodily form in the bodily arms of a woman. And the star remained above the statue of Pege, called the Celestial, until the wise men came forth, and then it went with them.

And then, in the depth of evening, Dionysus appeared in the temple, unaccompanied by the Satyrs, and said to the images: Pege is not one of us, but stands far above us, in that she gives birth to a man whose conception is in divine fashion. O priest Prupupius! What dost thou tarrying here? An action, indicated in writings of old, has come upon us, and we shall be convicted as false by a person of power and energy. Wherein we have been deceivers, we have been deceivers; and wherein we have ruled, we have ruled. No longer give we oracular responses. Gone from us is our honor. Without glory and reward are we become. There is One, and One only, who receives again at the hands of all His proper honor. For the rest, be not disturbed. No longer shall the Persians exact tribute of earth and sky. For He who established these things is at hand, to bring practical tribute to Him who sent Him, to renew the ancient image, and to put image with image, and bring the dissimilar to similarity. Heaven rejoices with earth, and earth itself exults at receiving matter of exultation from heaven. Things which have not happened above, have happened on earth beneath. He whom the order of the blessed has not seen, is seen by the order of the miserable. Flame threatens those; dew attends these. To Myria is given the blessed lot of bearing Pege in Bethlehem, and of conceiving grace of grace. Judea has seen its bloom, and this country is fading. To Gentiles and aliens, salvation is come; to the wretched, relief is ministered abundantly. With right do women dance, and say, Lady Pege, Spring-bearer, thou mother of the heavenly constellation. Thou cloud that brings us dew after heat, remember thy dependents, O mistress.

The king then, without delay, sent some of the Magi under his dominion with gifts, the star showing them the way. And when they returned, they narrated to the men of that time those same things which were also written on the plates of gold, and which were to the following effect:—

When we came to Jerusalem, the sign, together with our arrival, roused all the people. How is this, say they, that wise men of the Persians are here, and that along with them there is this strange stellar phenomenon? And the chief of the Jews interrogated us in this way: What is this that attends you, and with what purpose are you here? And we said: He whom ye call Messias is born. And they were confounded, and dared not withstand us. But they said to us, By the justice of Heaven, tell us what ye know of this matter. And we made answer to them: Ye labor under unbelief; and neither without an oath nor with an oath do ye believe us, but ye follow your own heedless counsel. For the Christ, the Son of the Most High, is born, and He is the subverter of your law and synagogues. And therefore is it that, struck with this most excellent response as with a dart, ye hear in bitterness this name which has come upon you suddenly. And they then, taking counsel together, urged us to accept their gifts, and tell to none that such an event had taken place in that land of theirs, lest, as they say, *a revolt rise against us*. But we replied: We have brought gifts in His honor, with the view of proclaiming those mighty things which we know to have happened in our country on occasion of His birth; and do ye bid us take your bribes, and conceal the things which have been communicated to us by the Divinity who is above the heavens, and neglect the commandments of our proper King? And after urging many considerations on us, they gave the matter up. And when the king of Judea sent for us and had some converse with us, and put to us certain questions as to the statements we made to him, we acted in the same manner, until he was thoroughly enraged at our replies. We left him accordingly, without giving any greater heed to him than to any common person.

And we came to that place then to which we were sent, and saw the mother and the child, the star indicating to us the royal babe. And we said to the mother: What art thou named, O renowned mother? And she says: Mary, masters. And we said to her: Whence art thou sprung? And she replies: From this district of the Bethlehemites. Then said we: Hast thou not had a husband? And she answers: I was only betrothed with a view to the marriage covenant, my thoughts being far removed from this. For I had no mind to come to this. And while I was giving very little concern to it, when a certain Sabbath dawned, and straightway at the rising of the sun, an angel appeared to me bringing me suddenly the glad tidings of a son. And in trouble I cried out, Be it not so to me, Lord, for I have not a husband. And he persuaded me to believe, that by the will of God I should have this son.

Then said we to her: Mother, mother, all the gods of the Persians have called thee blessed. Thy glory is great; for thou art exalted above all women of renown, and thou art shown to be more queenly than all queens.

The child, moreover, was seated on the ground, being, as she said, in His second year, and having in part the likeness of His mother. And she had long hands, and a body somewhat delicate; and her color was like that of ripe wheat; and she was of a round face, and had her hair bound up. And as we had along with us a servant skilled in painting from the life, we brought with us to our country a likeness of them both; and it was placed by our hand in the sacred temple, with this inscription on it: To Jove the Sun, the mighty God, the King of Jesus, the power of Persia dedicated this.

And taking the child up, each of us in turn, and bearing Him in our arms, we saluted Him and worshipped Him, and presented to Him gold, and myrrh, and frankincense, ad- dressing Him thus: We gift Thee with Thine own, O Jesus, Ruler of heaven. Ill would things unordered be ordered, wert Thou not at hand. In no other way could things heavenly be brought into conjunction with things earthly, but by Thy descent. Such service cannot be discharged, if only the servant is sent us, as when the Master Himself is present; neither can so much be achieved when the king sends only his satraps to war, as when the king is there himself. It became the wisdom of Thy system, that Thou shouldst deal in this manner with men.

And the child leaped and laughed at our caresses and words. And when we had bidden the mother farewell, and when she had shown us honor, and we had testified to her the reverence which became us, we came again to the place in which we lodged. And at eventide there appeared to us one of a terrible and fearful countenance, saying: Get ye out quickly, lest ye be taken in a snare. And we in terror said: And who is he, O divine leader, that plotted against so august an embassage? And he replied: Herod; but get you up straightway and depart in safety and peace.

And we made speed to depart thence in all earnestness; and we reported in Jerusalem all that we had seen. Behold, then, the great things that we have told you regarding Christ; and we saw Christ our Savior, who was made known as both God and man. To Him be the glory and the power unto the ages of the ages. Amen.

III.—The Extant Fragments of the Five Books of the Chronography of Julius Africanus.

I.
On the Mythical Chronology of the Egyptians and Chaldeans.

The Egyptians, indeed, with their boastful notions of their own antiquity, have put forth a sort of account of it by the hand of their astrologers in cycles and myriads of years; which some of those who have had the repute of studying such subjects profoundly have in a summary way called lunar years; and inclining no less than others to the mythical, *they think they* fall in with the eight or nine thousands of years which the Egyptian priests in Plato falsely reckon up to Solon.

(*And after some other matter:*)

For why should I speak of the three myriad years of the Phoenicians, or of the follies of the Chaldeans, their forty-eight myriads? For the Jews, deriving their origin from them as descendants of Abraham, having been taught a modest mind, and one such as becomes men, together with the truth by the spirit of Moses, have handed down to us, by their extant Hebrew histories, the number of 5500 years as the period up to the advent of the Word of salvation, that was announced to the world in the time of the sway of the Cesar's.

II.

When men multiplied on the earth, the angels of heaven came together with the daughters of men. In some copies I found "the sons of God." What is meant by the Spirit, in my opinion, is that the descendants of Seth are called the sons of God on account of the righteous men and patriarchs who have sprung from him, even down to the Savior Himself; but that the descendants of Cain are named the seed of men, as having nothing divine in them, on account of the wickedness of their race and the inequality of their nature, being a mixed people, and having stirred the indignation of God. But if it is thought that these refer to angels, we must take them to be those who deal with magic and jugglery, who taught the women the motions of the stars and the knowledge of things celestial, by whose power they conceived the giants as their children, by whom wickedness came to its height on the earth, until God decreed that the whole race of the living should perish in their impiety by the deluge.

III.

Adam, when 230 years old, begets Seth; and after living other 700 years he died, that is, a second death.

Seth, when 205 years old, begot Enos; from Adam therefore to the birth of Enos there are 435 years in all.

Enos, when 190 years old, begets Cainan.

Cainan again, when 170 years old, begets Malaleel;

And Malaleel, when 165 years old; begets Jared;

And Jared, when 162 years old, begets Enoch;

And Enoch, when 165 years old, begets Mathusala; and having pleased God, after a life of other 200 years, he was not found.

Mathusala, when 187 years old, begot Lamech.

Lamech, when 188 years old, begets Noe.

IV.

On the Deluge.

God decreed to destroy the whole race of the living by a flood, having threatened that men should not survive beyond 120 years. Nor let it be deemed a matter of difficulty, because some lived afterwards a longer period than that. For the space of time meant was 100 years up to the flood in the case of the sinners of that time; for they were 20 years old. God instructed Noe, who pleased him on account of his righteousness, to prepare an ark; and when it was finished, there entered it Noe himself and his sons, his wife and his daughters-in-law, and firstlings of every living creature, with a view to the duration of the race. And Noe was 600 years old when the flood came on. And when the water abated, the ark settled on the mountains of Ararat, which we know to be in Parthia; but some say that they are at Celænæ of Phrygia, and I have seen both places. And the flood prevailed for a year, and then the earth became dry. And they came out of the ark in pairs, as may be found, and not in the manner in which they had entered, viz., distinguished according to their species, and were blessed by God. And each of these things indicates something useful to us.

V.

Noe was 600 years old when the flood came on. From Adam, therefore, to Noe and the flood, are 2262 years.

VI.

And after the flood, Sem begot Arphaxad.

Arphaxad, when 135 years old, begets Sala in the year 2397.

Sala, when 130 years old, begets Heber in the year 2527.

Heber, when 134 years old, begets Phalec in the year 2661, so called because the earth was divided in his days.

Phalec, when 130 years old, begot Ragan, and after living other 209 years died.

VII.

In the year of the world 3277, Abraham entered the promised land of Canaan.

VIII.

Of Abraham.

From this rises the appellation of the *Hebrews*. For the word *Hebrews* is interpreted to mean *those who migrate across*, viz., who crossed the Euphrates with Abraham; and it is not derived, as some think, from the fore-mentioned Heber. From the flood and Noe, therefore, to Abraham's entrance into the promised land, there are in all 1015 years; and from Adam, in 20 generations 3277 years.

X.
Of the Patriarch Jacob.

1. The shepherd's tent belonging to Jacob, which was preserved at Edessa to the time of Antonine Emperor of the Romans, was destroyed by a thunderbolt.

2. Jacob, being displeased at what had been done by Symeon and Levi at Shecem against the people of the country, on account of the violation of their sister, buried at Shecem the gods which he had with him near a rock under the wonderful terebinth, which up to this day is reverenced by the neighboring people in honor of the patriarchs, and removed thence to Bethel. By the trunk of this terebinth there was an altar on which the inhabitants of the country offered *ectenæ* in their general assemblies; and though it seemed to be burned, it was not consumed. Near it is the tomb of Abraham and Isaac. And some say that the staff of one of the angels who were entertained by Abraham was planted there.

XI.

From Adam, therefore, to the death of Joseph, according to this book, are 23 generations, and 3563 years.

XII.

From this record, therefore, we affirm that Ogygus, from whom the first flood (in Attica) derived its name, and who was saved when many perished, lived at the time of the exodus of the people from Egypt along with Moses. (*After a break*): And after Ogygus, on account of the vast destruction caused by the flood, the present land of Attica remained without a king till the time of Cecrops, 189 years. Philochorus, however, affirms that Ogygus, Actæus, or whatever other fictitious name is adduced, never existed. (*After another break*): From Ogygus to Cyrus, as from Moses to his time, are 1235 years.

XIII.

1. Up to the time of the Olympiads there is no certain history among the Greeks, all things before that date being confused, and in no way consistent with each other. But these *Olympiads* were thoroughly investigated by many, as the Greeks made up the records of their history not according to long spaces, but in periods of four years. For which reason I shall select the most remarkable of the mythical narratives before the time of the first Olympiad, and rapidly run over them. But those after that period, at least those that are notable, I shall take together, Hebrew events in connection with Greek, according to their dates, examining carefully the affairs of the Hebrews, and touching more cursorily on those of the Greeks; and my plan will be as follows: Taking up some single event in Hebrew history synchronous with another in Greek history, and keeping by it as the main subject, subtracting or adding as may seem needful in the narrative, I shall note what Greek or Persian of note, or remarkable personage of any other nationality, flourished at the date of that event in Hebrew history; and thus I may perhaps attain the object which I propose to myself.

2. The most famous exile that befell the Hebrews, then—to wit, when they were led captive by Nabuchodonosor king of Babylon—lasted 70 years, as Jeremias had prophesied. Berosus the Babylonian, moreover, makes mention of Nabuchodonosor. And after the 70 years of captivity, Cyrus became king of the Persians at the time of the 55th Olympiad, as may be ascertained from the *Bibliothecæ* of Diodorus and the histories of Thallus and Castor, and also from Polybius and Phlegon, and others besides these, who have made the Olympiads a subject of study. For the date is a matter of agreement among them all. And Cyrus then, in the first year of his reign, which was the first year of the 55th Olympiad, effected the first partial restoration of the people by the hand of Zorobabel, with whom also was Jesus the son of Josedec, since the period of 70 years was now fulfilled, as is narrated in Esdra the Hebrew historian. The narratives of the beginning of the sovereignty of Cyrus and the end of the captivity accordingly coincide. And thus, according to the reckoning of the Olympiads, there will be found a like harmony of events even to our time. And by following this, we shall also make the other narratives fit in with each other in the same manner.

3. But if the Attic time-reckoning is taken as the standard for affairs prior to these, then from Ogygus, who was believed by them to be an autochthon, in whose time also the first great flood took place in Attica, while Phoroneus reigned over the Argives, as Acusilaus relates, up to the date of the first Olympiad, from which period the Greeks thought they could fix dates accurately, there are altogether 1020 years; which number both coincides with the above-mentioned, and will be established by

what follows. For these things are also recorded by the Athenian historians Hellanicus and Philochorus, who record Attic affairs; and by Castor and Thallus, who record Syrian affairs; and by Diodorus, who writes a universal history in his *Bibliothecæ*; and by Alexander Polyhistor, and by some of our own time, yet more carefully, and by all the Attic writers. Whatever narrative of note, therefore, meets us in these 1020 years, shall be given in its proper place.

4. In accordance with this writing, therefore, we affirm that Ogygus, who gave his name to the first flood, and was saved when many perished, lived at the time of the exodus of the people from Egypt along with Moses. And this we make out in the following manner. From Ogygus up to the first Olympiad already mentioned, it will be shown that there are 1020 years; and from the first Olympiad to the first year of the 55th, that is the first year of King Cyrus, which was also the end of the captivity, are 217 years. From Ogygus, therefore, to Cyrus are 1237. And if one carries the calculation backwards from the end of the captivity, there are 1237 years. Thus, by analysis, the same period is found to the first year of the exodus of Israel under Moses from Egypt, as from the 55th Olympiad to Ogygus, who founded Eleusis. And from this point we get a more notable beginning for Attic chronography.

5. So much, then, for the period prior to Ogygus. And at his time Moses left Egypt. And we demonstrate in the following manner how reliable is the statement that this happened at that date. From the exodus of Moses up to Cyrus, who reigned after the captivity, are 1237 years. For the remaining years of Moses are 40. The years of Jesus, who led the people after him, are 25; those of the

elders, who were judges after Jesus, are 30; those of the judges, whose history is given in the book of Judges, are 490; those of the priests Eli and Samuel are 90; those of the successive kings of the Hebrews are 490. *Then come the 70 years of the captivity*, 1110 the last year of which was the first year of the reign of Cyrus, as we have already said.

6. And from Moses, then, to the first Olympiad there are 1020 years, as to the first year of the 55th Olympiad from the same are 1237, in which enumeration the reckoning of the Greeks coincides with us. And after Ogygus, by reason of the vast destruction caused by the flood, the present land of Attica remained without a king up to Cecrops, a period of 189 years. For Philochorus asserts that the Actæus who is said to have succeeded Ogygus, or whatever other fictitious names are adduced, never existed. *And again*: From Ogygus, therefore, to Cyrus, *says he*, the same period is reckoned as from Moses to the same date, viz., 1237 years; and some of the Greeks also record that Moses lived at that same time. Polemo, for instance, in the first book of his *Greek History*, says: In the time of Apis, son of Phoroneus, a division of the army of the Egyptians left Egypt, and settled in the Palestine called Syrian, not far from Arabia: these are evidently those who were with Moses. And Apion the son of Poseidonius, the most laborious of grammarians, in his book *Against the Jews*, and in the fourth book of his *History*, says that in the time of Inachus king of Argos, when Amosis reigned over Egypt, the Jews revolted under the leadership of Moses. And Herodotus also makes mention of this revolt, and of Amosis, in his second book, and in a certain way also of the Jews themselves, reckoning them among the circumcised and

calling them the Assyrians of Palestine, perhaps through Abraham. And Ptolemy the Mendesian, who narrates the history of the Egyptians from the earliest times, gives the same account of all these things; so that among them in general there is no difference worth notice in the chronology.

7. It should be observed, further, that all the legendary accounts which are deemed specially remarkable by the Greeks by reason of their antiquity, are found to belong to a period posterior to Moses; such as their floods and conflagrations, Prometheus, Io, Europa, the Sparti, the abduction of Proserpine, their mysteries, their legislations, the deeds of Dionysus, Perseus, the Argonauts, the Centaurs, the Minotaur, the affairs of Troy, the labors of Hercules, the return of the Heraclidæ, the Ionian migration and the Olympiads. And it seemed good to me to give an account, especially of the before-noted period of the Attic sovereignty, as I intend to narrate the history of the Greeks side by side with that of the Hebrews. For anyone will be able, if he only start from my position, to make out the reckoning equally well with me. Now, in the first year of that period of 1020 years, stretching from Moses and Ogygus to the first Olympiad, the Passover and the exodus of the Hebrews from Egypt took place, and also in Attica the flood of Ogygus. And that is according to reason. For when the Egyptians were being smitten in the anger of God with hail and storms, it was only to be expected that certain parts of the earth should suffer with them; and, in especial, it was but to be expected that the Athenians should participate in such calamity with the Egyptians, since they were supposed to be a colony from them, as Theopompus alleges in his *Tricarenus*, and others besides

him. The intervening period has been passed by, as no remarkable event is recorded during it among the Greeks. But after 94 years Prometheus arose, according to some, who was fabulously reported to have formed men; for being a wise man, he transformed them from the state of extreme rudeness to culture.

XIV.

Æschylus, the son of Agamestor, ruled the Athenians twenty-three years, in whose time Joatham reigned in Jerusalem.

And our canon brings Joatham king of Juda within the first Olympiad.

XV.

And Africanus, in the third book of his History, writes: Now the first Olympiad recorded—which, however, was really the fourteenth—was the period when Coroebus was victor; at that time Ahaz was in the first year of his reign in Jerusalem. *Then in the fourth book he says*: It is therefore with the first year of the reign of Ahaz that we have shown the first Olympiad to fall in.

XVI.

On the Seventy Weeks of Daniel.

1. This passage, therefore, as it stands thus, touches on many marvelous things. At present, however, I shall speak only of those things in it which bear upon chronology, and matters connected therewith. That the passage speaks then of the advent of Christ, who was to manifest Himself after seventy weeks, is evident. For in the Savior's time, or from Him, are transgressions abrogated, and sins brought to an end. And through

remission, moreover, are iniquities, along with offences, blotted out by expiation; and an everlasting righteousness is preached, different from that which is by the law, and visions and prophecies (are) until John, and the Most Holy is anointed. For before the advent of the Savior these things were not yet, and were therefore only looked for. And the beginning of the numbers, that is, of the seventy weeks which make up 490 years, the angel instructs us to take from the going forth of the commandment to answer and to build Jerusalem. And this happened in the twentieth year of the reign of Artaxerxes king of Persia. For Nehemiah his cup-bearer besought him, and received the answer that Jerusalem should be built. And the word went forth commanding these things; for up to that time the city was desolate. For when Cyrus, after the seventy years' captivity, gave free permission to all to return who desired it, some of them under the leadership of Jesus the high priest and Zorobabel, and others after these under the leadership of Esdra, returned, but were prevented at first from building the temple, and from surrounding the city with a wall, on the plea that that had not been commanded.

2. It remained in this position, accordingly, until Nehemiah and the reign of Artaxerxes, and the 115th year of the sovereignty of the Persians. And from the capture of Jerusalem that makes 185 years. And at that time King Artaxerxes gave order that the city should be built; and Nehemiah being dispatched, superintended the work, and the street and the surrounding wall were built, as had been prophesied. And reckoning from that point, we make up seventy weeks to the time of Christ. For if we begin to reckon from any other point, and not from this, the periods will not correspond, and very many odd results

will meet us. For if we begin the calculation of the seventy weeks from Cyrus and the first restoration, there will be upwards of one hundred years too many, and there will be a larger number if we begin from the day on which the angel gave the prophecy to Daniel, and a much larger number still if we begin from the commencement of the captivity. For we find the sovereignty of the Persians comprising a period of 230 years, and that of the Macedonians extending over 370 years, and from that to the 16th year of Tiberius Cæsar is a period of about 60 years.

4. It is by calculating from Artaxerxes, therefore, up to the time of Christ that the seventy weeks are made up, according to the numeration of the Jews. For from Nehemiah, who was dispatched by Artaxerxes to build Jerusalem in the 115th year of the Persian empire, and the 4th year of the 83d Olympiad, and the 20th year of the reign of Artaxerxes himself, up to this date, which was the second year of the 202d Olympiad, and the 16th year of the reign of Tiberius Cæsar, there are reckoned 475 years, which make 490 according to the Hebrew numeration, as they measure the years by the course of the moon; so that, as is easy to show, their year consists of 354 days, while the solar year has 365¼ days. For the latter exceeds the period of twelve months, according to the moon's course, by 11¼ days. Hence the Greeks and the Jews insert three intercalary months every 8 years. For 8 times 11¼ days makes up 3 months. Therefore 475 years make 59 periods of 8 years each, and 3 months besides. But since thus there are 3 intercalary months every 8 years, we get thus 15 years *minus* a few days; and these being added to the 475 years, make up in all the 70 weeks.

XVII.

On the Fortunes of Hyrcanus and Antigonus, and on Herod, Augustus, Antony, and Cleopatra, in Abstract.

1. Octavius Sebastus, or, as the Romans call him, Augustus, the adopted son of Caius, on returning to Rome from Apollonias in Epirus, where he was educated, possessed himself of the first place in the government. And Antony afterwards obtained the rule of Asia and the districts beyond. In his time the Jews accused Herod; but he put the deputies to death, and restored Herod to his government. Afterwards, however, along with Hyrcanus and Phasælus his brother, he was driven out, and betook himself in flight to Antony. And as the Jews would not receive him, an obstinate battle took place; and in a short time after, as he had conquered in battle, he also drove out Antigonus, who had returned. And Antigonus fled to Herod the Parthian king, and was restored by the help of his son Pacorus, which help was given on his promising to pay 1000 talents of gold. And Herod then in his turn had to flee, while Phasælus was slain in battle, and Hyrcanus was surrendered alive to Antigonus. And after cutting off his ears, that he might be disqualified for the priesthood, he gave him to the Parthians to lead into captivity; for he scrupled to put him to death, as he was a relation of his own. And Herod, on his expulsion, betook himself first to Malichus king of the Arabians; and when he did not receive him, through fear of the Parthians, he went away to Alexandria to Cleopatra. That was the 185th Olympiad. Cleopatra having put to death her brother, who was her consort in the government, and being then summoned by Antony to Cilicia to make her defense, committed the care of the sovereignty to Herod; and as he requested that he should not be entrusted with anything

until he was restored to his own government, she took him with her and went to Antony. And as he was smitten with love for the princess, they dispatched Herod to Rome to Octavius Augustus, who, on behalf of Antipater, Herod's father, and on behalf of Herod himself, and also because Antigonus was established as king by the help of the Parthians, gave a commission to the generals in Palestine and Syria to restore him to his government. And in concert with Sosius he waged war against Antigonus for a long time, and in manifold engagements. At that time also, Josephus, Herod's brother, died in his command. And Herod coming to Antony ...

2. For three years they besieged Antigonus, and then brought him alive to Antony. And Antony himself also proclaimed Herod as king, and gave him, in addition, the cities Hippus, Gadara, Gaza, Joppa, Anthedon, and a part of Arabia, Trachonitis, and Auranitis, and Sacia, and Gaulanitis; and besides these, also the procuratorship of Syria. Herod was declared king of the Jews by the senate and Octavius Augustus, and reigned 34 years. Antony, when about to go on an expedition against the Parthians, slew Antigonus the king of the Jews, and gave Arabia to Cleopatra; and passing over into the territory of the Parthians, sustained a severe defeat, losing the greater part of his army. That was in the 186th Olympiad. Octavius Augustus led the forces of Italy and all the West against Antony, who refused to return to Rome through fear, on account of his failure in Parthia, and through his love for Cleopatra. And Antony met him with the forces of Asia. Herod, however, like a shrewd fellow, and one who waits upon the powerful, sent a double set of letters, and dispatched his army to sea, charging his generals to watch the issue of events. And when the victory was decided,

and when Antony, after sustaining two naval defeats, had fled to Egypt along with Cleopatra, they who bore the letters delivered to Augustus those which they had been keeping secretly for Antony. And on Herod falls...

3. Cleopatra shut herself up in a mausoleum, and made away with herself, employing the wild asp as the instrument of death. At that time Augustus captured Cleopatra's sons, Helios and Selene, on their flight to the Thebaid. Nicopolis was founded opposite Actium, and the games called Actia were instituted. On the capture of Alexandria, Cornelius Gallus was sent as first governor of Egypt, and he destroyed the cities of the Egyptians that refused obedience. Up to this time the Lagidæ ruled; and the whole duration of the Macedonian empire after the subversion of the Persian power was 298 years. Thus is made up the whole period from the foundation of the Macedonian empire to its subversion in the time of the Ptolemies, and under Cleopatra, the last of these, the date of which event is the 11th year of the monarchy and empire of the Romans, and the 4th year of the 187th Olympiad. Altogether, from Adam 5472 years are reckoned.

4. After the taking of Alexandria the 188th Olympiad began. Herod founded anew the city of the Gabinii, the ancient Samaria, and called it Sebaste; and having erected its seaport, the tower of Strato, into a city, he named it Caesarea after the same, and raised in each a temple in honor of Octavius. And afterwards he founded Antipatris in the Lydian plain, so naming it after his father, and settled in it the people about Sebaste, whom he had dispossessed of their land. He founded also other cities; and to the Jews he was severe, but to other nations most urbane.

It was now the 189th Olympiad, which (Olympiad) in the year that had the bissextile day, the 6th day before the Calends of March,—i.e., the 24th of February,—corresponded with the 24th year of the era of Antioch, whereby the year was determined in its proper limits.

XVIII.
On the Circumstances Connected with Our Savior's Passion and His Life-Giving Resurrection.

1. As to His works severally, and His cures effected upon body and soul, and the mysteries of His doctrine, and the resurrection from the dead, these have been most authoritatively set forth by His disciples and apostles before us. On the whole world there pressed a most fearful darkness; and the rocks were rent by an earthquake, and many places in Judea and other districts were thrown down. This darkness Thallus, in the third book of his *History*, calls, as appears to me without reason, an eclipse of the sun. For the Hebrews celebrate the Passover on the 14th day according to the moon, and the passion of our Savior falls on the day before the Passover; but an eclipse of the sun takes place only when the moon comes under the sun. And it cannot happen at any other time but in the interval between the first day of the new moon and the last of the old, that is, at their junction: how then should an eclipse be supposed to happen when the moon is almost diametrically opposite the sun? Let that opinion pass however; let it carry the majority with it; and let this portent of the world be deemed an eclipse of the sun, like others a portent only to the eye. Phlegon records that, in the time of Tiberius Cæsar, at full moon, there was a full eclipse of the sun

from the sixth hour to the ninth—manifestly that one of which we speak. But what has an eclipse in common with an earthquake, the rending rocks, and the resurrection of the dead, and so great a perturbation throughout the universe? Surely no such event as this is recorded for a long period. But it was a darkness induced by God, because the Lord happened then to suffer. And calculation makes out that the period of 70 weeks, as noted in Daniel, is completed at this time.

2. From Artaxerxes, moreover, 70 weeks are reckoned up to the time of Christ, according to the numeration of the Jews. For from Nehemiah, who was sent by Artaxerxes to people Jerusalem, about the 120th year of the Persian empire, and in the 20th year of Artaxerxes himself, and the 4th year of the 83d Olympiad, up to this time, which was the 2d year of the 102d Olympiad, and the 16th year of the reign of Tiberius Cæsar, there are given 475 years, which make 490 Hebrew years, since they measure the years by the lunar month of 29½ days, as may easily be explained, the annual period according to the sun consisting of 365¼ days, while the lunar period of 12 months has 11¼ days less. For which reason the Greeks and the Jews insert three intercalary months every eight years. For 8 times 11¼ days make 3 months. The 475 years, therefore, contain 59 periods of 8 years and three months over: thus, the three intercalary months for every 8 years being added, we get 15 years, and these together with the 475 years make 70 weeks. Let no one now think us unskilled in the calculations of astronomy, when we fix without further ado the number of days at 365¼. For it is not in ignorance of the truth, but rather by reason of exact study,1127 that we have stated our opinion so shortly. But

let what follows also be presented as in outline to those who endeavor to inquire minutely into all things.

3. Each year in the general consists of 365 days; and the space of a day and night being divided into nineteen parts, we have also five of these. And in saying that the year consists of 365¼ days, and there being the five nineteenth parts...to the 475 there are 6¼ days. Furthermore, we find, according to exact computation, that the lunar month has 29½ days....And these come to 1130 a little time. Now it happens that from the 20th year of the reign of Artaxerxes (as it is given in Ezra among the Hebrews), which, according to the Greeks, was the 4th year of the 80th Olympiad, to the 16th year of Tiberius Cæsar, which was the second year of the 102d Olympiad, there are in all the 475 years already noted, which in the Hebrew system make 490 years, as has been previously stated, that is, 70 weeks, by which period the time of Christ's advent was measured in the announcement made to Daniel by Gabriel. And if anyone thinks that the 15 Hebrew years added to the others involve us in an error of 10, nothing at least which cannot be accounted for has been introduced. And the 1½ week which we suppose must be added to make the whole number, meets the question about the 15 years, and removes the difficulty about the time; and that the prophecies are usually put forth in a somewhat symbolic form, is quite evident.

4. As far, then, as is in our power, we have taken the Scripture, I think, correctly; especially seeing that the preceding section about the vision seems to state the whole matter shortly, its first words being, "In the third year of the reign of Belshazzar," where he prophesies of the subversion of the Persian power by the Greeks, which

empires are symbolized in the prophecy under the figures of the ram and the goat respectively. "The sacrifice," he says, "shall be abolished, and the holy places shall be made desolate, so as to betrodden under foot; which things shall be determined within 2300 days." For if we take the day as a month, just as elsewhere in prophecy days are taken as years, and in different places are used in different ways, reducing the period in the same way as has been done above to Hebrew months, we shall find the period fully made out to the 20th year of the reign of Artaxerxes, from the capture of Jerusalem. For there are given thus 185 years, and one year falls to be added to these—the year in which Nehemiah built the wall of the city. In 186 years, therefore, we find 2300 Hebrew months, as 8 years have in addition 3 intercalary months. From Artaxerxes, again, in whose time the command went forth that Jerusalem should be built, there are 70 weeks. These matters, however, we have discussed by themselves, and with greater exactness, in our book *On the Weeks and this Prophecy*. But I am amazed that the Jews deny that the Lord has yet come, and that the followers of Marcion refuse to admit that His coming was predicted in the prophecies when the Scriptures display the matter so openly to our view. *And after something else*: The period, then, to the advent of the Lord from Adam and the creation is 5531 years, from which epoch to the 250th Olympiad there are 192 years, as has been shown above.

XIX.

For we who both know the measure of those words, and are not ignorant of the grace of faith, give thanks to the Father, who has bestowed on us His creatures Jesus Christ the Savior of all, and our Lord; to whom be glory and majesty, with the Holy Spirit, forever.

IV.—The Passion of St. Symphorosa and Her Seven Sons.

The text is given from the edition of Ruinart. His preface, which Migne also cites, is as follows: "The narrative of the martyrdom of St. Symphorosa and her seven sons, which we here publish, is ascribed in the mss. to Julius Africanus, a writer of the highest repute. And it may perhaps have been inserted in his books on *Chronography*,—a work which Eusebius (*Hist. Eccles.*, vi. 31) testifies to have been written with the greatest care, since in these he detailed the chief events in history from the foundation of the world to the times of the Emperor Heliogabalus. As that work, however, is lost, that this narrative is really to be ascribed to Africanus, I would not venture positively to assert, although at the same time there seems no ground for doubting its genuineness. We print it, moreover, from the editions of Mombritius, Surius, and Cardulus, collated with two Colbert mss. and one in the library of the Sorbonne. The occasion for the death of these saints was found in the vicinity of that most famous palace which was built by Adrian at his country seat at Tiber, according to Spartianus. For when the emperor gave orders that this palace, which he had built for his pleasure, should be purified by some piacular ceremonies, the priests seized this opportunity for accusing Symphorosa, alleging that the gods would not be satisfied until Symphorosa should either sacrifice to them or be herself sacrificed; which last thing was done by

Hadrian, whom, from many others of his deeds, we know to have been exceedingly superstitious, about the year of Christ 120, that is, about the beginning of his reign, at which period indeed, as Dio Cassius observes, that emperor put a great number to death. The memory of these martyrs, moreover, is celebrated in all the most ancient martyrologies, although they assign different days for it. The Roman, along with Notker, fixes their festival for the 18th July, Rabanus for the 21st of the same month, Usuardus and Ado for the 21st June. In the Tiburtine road there still exists the rubbish of an old church, as Aringhi states (*Rom. Subter.*, iv. 17), which was consecrated to God under their name, and which still retains the title, *To the Seven Brothers*. I have no doubt that it was built in that place to which the pontiffs in the *Acta*, sec. iv., gave the name, *To the Seven Biothanati*, i.e., those cut off by a violent death, as Baronius remarks, at the year 138." So far Ruinart: see also Tillemont, *Mém. Eccles.*, ii. pp. 241 and 595; and the Bollandists, *Act. S.S. Junii*, vol. iv. p. 350.

    1. When Adrian had built a palace, and wished to dedicate it by that wicked ceremonial, and began to seek responses by sacrifices to idols, and to the demons that dwell in idols, they replied, and said: "The widow Symphorosa, with her seven sons, wounds us day by day in invoking her God. If she therefore, together with her sons, shall offer sacrifice, we promise to make good all that you ask." Then Adrian ordered her to be seized, along with her sons, and advised them in courteous terms to consent to offer sacrifice to the idols. To him, however, the blessed Symphorosa answered: "My husband Getulius, together with his brother Amantius, when they were tribunes in thy service, suffered different

punishments for the name of Christ, rather than consent to sacrifice to idols, and, like good athletes, they overcame thy demons in death. For, rather than be prevailed on, they chose to be beheaded, and suffered death: which death, being endured for the name of Christ, gained them temporal ignominy indeed among men of this earth, but everlasting honor and glory among the angels; and moving now among them, and exhibiting trophies of their sufferings, they enjoy eternal life with the King eternal in the heavens."

2. The Emperor Adrian said to the holy Symphorosa: "Either sacrifice thou along with thy sons to the omnipotent gods, or else I shall cause thee to be sacrificed thyself, together with thy sons." The blessed Symphorosa answered: "And whence is this great good to me, that I should be deemed worthy along with my sons to be offered as an oblation to God?" The Emperor Adrian said: "I shall cause thee to be sacrificed to my gods." The blessed Symphorosa replied: "Thy gods cannot take me in sacrifice; but if I am burned for the name of Christ, my God, I shall rather consume those demons of thine." The Emperor Adrian said: "Choose thou one of these alternatives: either sacrifice to my gods, or perish by an evil death." The blessed Symphorosa replied: "Thou thinks that my mind can be altered by some kind of terror; whereas I long to rest with my husband Getulius, whom thou didst put to death for Christ's name." Then the Emperor Adrian ordered her to be led away to the temple of Hercules, and there first to be beaten with blows on the cheek, and afterwards to be suspended by the hair. But when by no argument and by no terror could he divert her from her good resolution, he ordered her to be thrown into the river with a large stone fastened to her neck. And her

brother Eugenius, principal of the district of Tiber, picked up her body, and buried it in a suburb of the same city.

3. Then, on another day, the Emperor Adrian ordered all her seven sons to be brought before him in company; and when he had challenged them to sacrifice to idols, and perceived that they yielded by no means to his threats and terrors, he ordered seven stakes to be fixed around the temple of Hercules, and commanded them to be stretched on the blocks there. And he ordered Crescens, the first, to be transfixed in the throat; and Julian, the second, to be stabbed in the breast; and Nemesius, the third, to be struck through the heart; and Primitivus, the fourth, to be wounded in the navel; and Justin, the fifth, to be struck through in the back with a sword; and Stracteus, the sixth, to be wounded in the side; and Eugenius, the seventh, to be cleft in twain from the head downwards.

4. The next day again the Emperor Adrian came to the temple of Hercules, and ordered their bodies to be carried off together, and cast into a deep pit; and the pontiffs gave to that place the name, *To the Seven Biothanati*. After these things the persecution ceased for a year and a half, in which period the holy bodies of all the martyrs were honored, and consigned with all care to tumuli erected for that purpose, and their names are written in the book of life. The natal day, moreover, of the holy martyrs of Christ, the blessed Symphorosa and her seven sons, Crescens, Julian, Nemesius, Primitivus, Justin, Stracteus, and Eugenius, is held on the 18th July. Their bodies rest on the Tiburtine road, at the eighth milestone from the city, under the kingship of our Lord Jesus Christ, to whom is honor and glory for ever and ever. Amen.

Elucidations.

I.

(Joseph the son of both, p. 127.)

The opinion that Luke's genealogy is that of *Mary* was unknown to Christian antiquity. In the fifteenth century it was first propounded by Latin divines to do honor (as they supposed) to the Blessed Virgin. It was first broached by Annius of Viterbo, a.d. 1502. Christian antiquity is agreed that:—

1. Both genealogies are those of Joseph.

2. That Joseph was the son of Jacob or of Heli, either by adoption, or because Jacob and
Heli were either own brothers or half-brothers; so that,—

3. On the death of one of the brothers, without issue, the surviving brother married his widow, who became the mother of Joseph by this marriage; so that Joseph was reckoned the son of Jacob and the son of Heli.1146

4. Joseph and Mary were of the same lineage, but the Hebrews did not reckon descent from the side of the woman. *For them* St. Luke's genealogy is the sufficient register of Christ's royal descent and official claim. St. Luke gives his *personal* pedigree, ascending to Adam, and identifying Him with the whole human race.

II.

(Conclusion, cap. xix. p. 138.)

On Jewish genealogies, note Dean Prideaux,1147 vol. i. p. 296, and compare Lardner, vol. ii. 129, *et alibi*. Stillingfleet1148 should not be overlooked in what he says of the *uncertainties* of heathen chronology.

Lardner repeatedly calls our author a "great man;" and his most valuable account, digested from divers ancient and modern writers, must be consulted by the student. Let us observe the books of Scripture which his citations attest, and the great value of his attestation of the two genealogies of our Lord. Lardner dates the Letter to Origen1150 a.d. 228 or 240, according to divers conjectures of the learned. He concludes with this beautiful tribute: "We may glory in Africanus as a Christian" among those "whose shining abilities rendered them the ornament of the age in which they lived,—men of unspotted characters, giving evident proofs of honesty and integrity."

Note.
_____

The valuable works of Africanus are found in vol. ix. of the Edinburgh edition, mixed up with the spurious *Decretals* and remnants of preceding volumes. I am unable to make out very clearly who is the translator, but infer that Drs. Roberts and Donaldson should be credited with this work.

Find this and other great works of the early Church Fathers at lighthousechristianpublishing.com.

Julius Africanus

Our Father who art in heaven, hallowed be
thy name.
Thy kingdom come, Thy will be done, on
earth as it is in heaven.
Give us this day our daily bread and
forgive us our trespasses as we forgive those who
trespass against us.
And lead us not into temptation, but deliver
us from evil, for Thy is the kingdom, the power
and the glory.

Amen

Hail Mary full of grace, the Lord is with thee. Blessed art thou amongst women and blessed is the fruit of thy womb Jesus. Holy Mary mother of God, pray for us sinners, now and the hour of our death.

www.ingramcontent.com/pod-product-compliance
Lightning Source LLC
Chambersburg PA
CBHW052207070526
44585CB00017B/2099